# Comiendo el Arcoiris
# Eating the Rainbow

Patricia Barrera Boyer

-Harlee and Hayden,

    gracias por comer el arcoíris conmigo.

© 2020 by Patricia Barrera Boyer
ISBN #978-1-7363128-0-3

Published by Mi Bici Bilingüe
 www.mibicibilingue.com
www.mybilingualbike.com

7760 E State Route 69
Suite C5-323
Prescott Valley, AZ 86314

# Free Coloring Pages and More!
# Paginas de Colorear, Gratis y Más!

Hi Friends,

Ask your parents to visit the link below for some free coloring pages that you can use to ask for yummy new foods to try!

Your friend,
 Patricia

https://mybilingualbike.com/coloring

Hola Amigos,

Pídele a sus padres a visitar el enlace para recibir unas paginas que puedes usar y para pedir unas comidas sabrosas para probar!

Tu amiga,
 Patricia

https://mibicibilingue.com/colorear

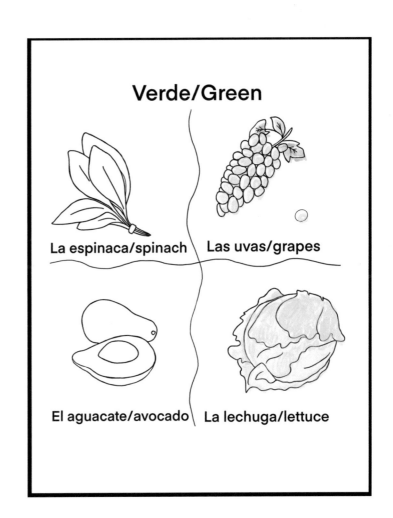

¡Hola! Me llamo Ceci.


Hi! My name is Ceci.

Me gusta comer comidas blancas como ...........

I like to eat foods that are white like..........

Mi abuelita dice, "Debes comer el arcoíris. Es muy sabroso."

My grandma says, "You should eat the rainbow. It's delicious ."

"¡Usted es muy chistosa, Abuelita! No puedo comer un arcoíris," Le respondo.

"You are very silly, Grandma! I can't eat a rainbow," I respond.

Abuelita dice, "Vamos a la tienda y yo te enseño."

Grandma says, "Let's go to the store and I will show you."

"¡Mira! Las comidas buenas tienen los colores del arcoíris. ¡Hay comidas rojas, anaranjadas, amarillas, verdes, azules, moradas, y violetas!" Dice Abuelita muy emocionada.

"Look! The foods that are good have the colors of the rainbow. There is red, orange, yellow, green, blue, purple, and violet!" Grandma says excitedly.

Abuelita me informa, "Esta semana vamos a comer comidas de un color diferente cada día."

Grandma informs me, "This week we are going to eat foods of a different color each day."

# Septiembre * September

| lunes | martes | miércoles | jueves | viernes | sábado | domingo |
|-------|--------|-----------|--------|---------|--------|---------|
| Monday | Tuesday | Wednesday | Thursday | Friday | Saturday | Sunday |

"El lunes vamos a comer las comidas rojas. Hay tomate, fresa, remolacha, y cereza."


"On Monday, we will eat foods that are red. There is tomato, strawberry, beet, and cherry."

"El martes vamos a comer las comidas anaranjadas. Hay naranja, camote, zanahoria, y albaricoque."


"On Tuesday, we will eat foods that are orange. There is an orange, sweet potato, carrot, and apricot."

"¡El miércoles vamos a comer las comidas amarillas! Hay piña, limón, plátano, y elote. "

"On Wednesday, we will eat foods that are yellow! There is pineapple, lemon, banana, and corn."

"El jueves vamos a comer las comidas verdes. Hay espinaca, uvas, aguacate, y lechuga."

"On Thursday, we will eat foods that are green. There is spinach, grape, avocado, and lettuce."

"El viernes vamos a comer comidas azules como arándanos y tortillitas de maíz azul."

"On Friday, we will eat foods that are blue like blueberries and blue corn tortilla chips."

"El sábado vamos a comer comidas moradas como las ciruelas pasas y los higos de nuestros árboles."

"On Saturday, we will eat foods that are purple like plums and figs from our fruit trees."

"El domingo vamos a comer comidas violetas como las uvas."

"On Sunday, we will eat foods that are violet like grapes."

"¡Abuelita, muchas gracias por mi semana del arcoíris! Mañana voy a compartir el arcoíris con mis amigas," Le digo a Abuelita.

"Grandma, thank you so much for my rainbow week! Tomorrow I will share the rainbow with my friends," I tell Grandma.

"¡Hola amigas! Quieren probar mi arcoíris? "

"Hi friends! Would you like to try my rainbow?"

Muchas gracias a mi esposo trabajador y lindo y a mis hijos cariñosos que son mi inspiración. Gracias a Erin y Blaine por todo tu ayuda técnica infatigable. Gracias a mi prima, Adrianne, que siempre me está aplaudiendo con cada paso. Gracias a mis comadres Debbie, Elia, Connie, Amber, y mi prima hermosa, Leticia, por todo tu apoyo y sabiduría en este proyecto. -P.B.B.


Many thanks to my wonderful, hard-working husband and my affectionate children, you are my inspiration. Thank you Erin and Blaine for your tireless technical assistance. Thank you to my cousin Adrianne who cheers me on with every step. Thank you to my "comadres" Debbie, Elia, Connie, Amber, and my beautiful cousin, Leticia, for all your support and wisdom on this project. -P.B.B.

# About the Author

Patricia Barrera Boyer is a bilingual speech-language pathologist who started her career working at La Rabida Children's Hospital in Chicago. She later continued her work in the public schools of Chicago and northern Illinois serving bilingual students in special education for 20 years. She grew up surrounded by two very large and loving Mexican-American families who loved eating, talking, and dancing. Currently, she is living in Northern Arizona with her family developing her creative self in illustration, cooking, and gardening.

Made in United States
Cleveland, OH
17 November 2024